EASY PIANO

FEB 1 0 2012

ADELE 21

ISBN 978-1-4584-1322-2

D1372943

HAL•LEONARD®
CORPORATION
7777 W. BLUEMOUND RD. P.O. BOX 13819 MILWAUKEE, WI 53213

Visit Hal Leonard Online at
www.halleonard.com

ROLLING IN THE DEEP

Words and Music by ADELE ADKINS
and PAUL EPWORTH

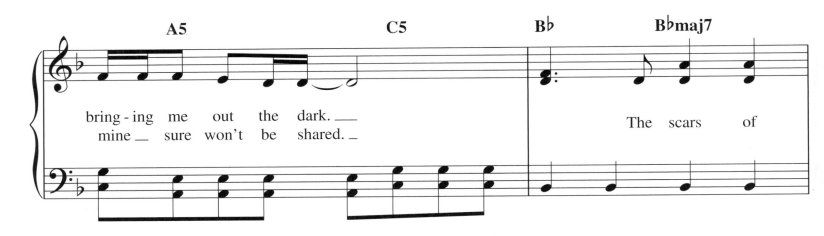

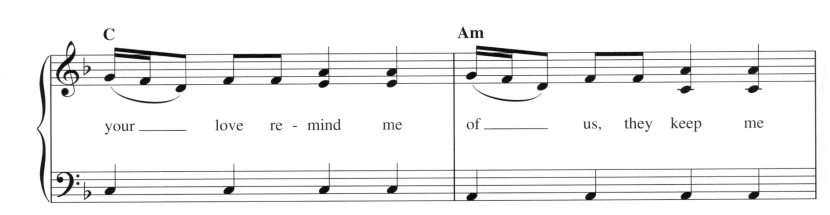

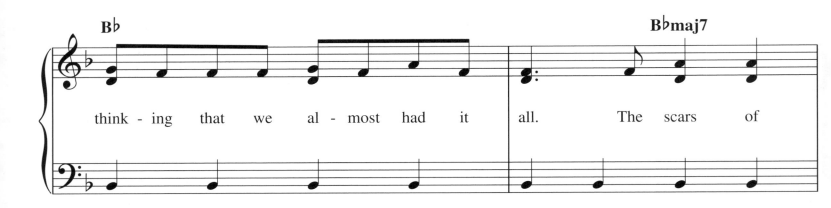

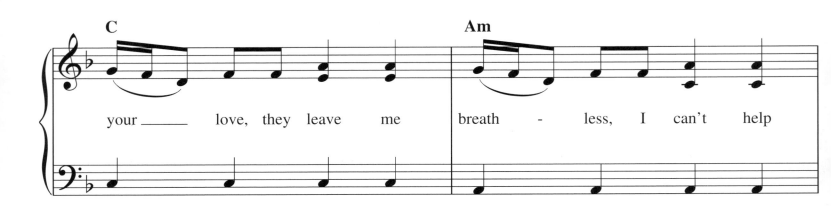

6

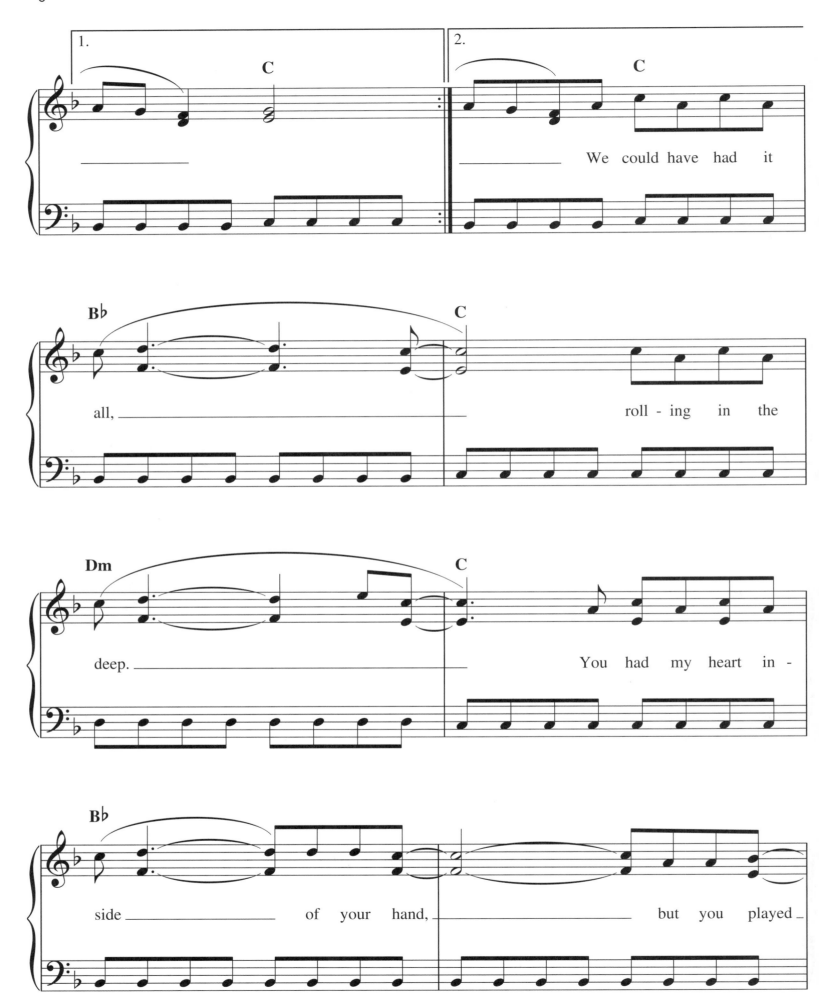

C7

it _____ with a beat - ing...

C

N.C.

Throw your soul _____ through ev - er - y o - pen door,

count your bless - ings to find what you look for. Turn my sor - row

in - to treas-ured gold. You pay me back in kind and reap just what you sow. ___

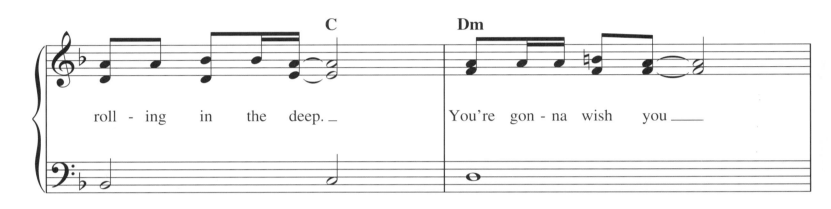

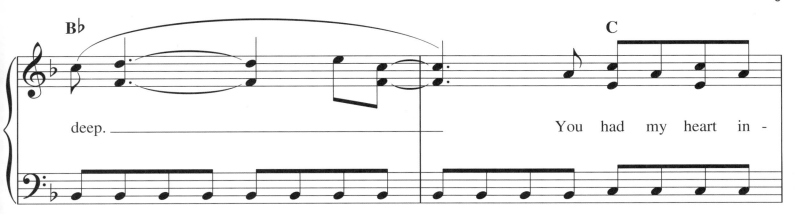

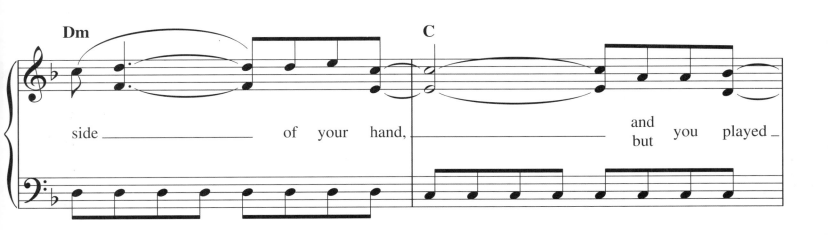

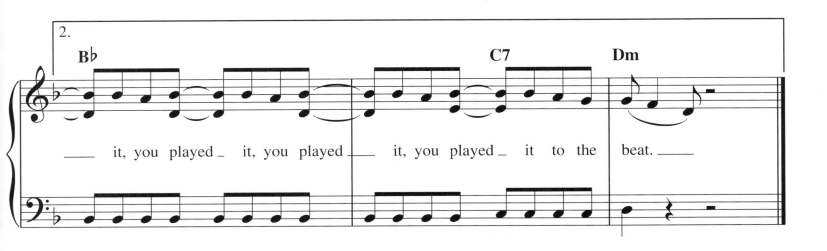

RUMOUR HAS IT

Words and Music by ADELE ADKINS
and RYAN TEDDER

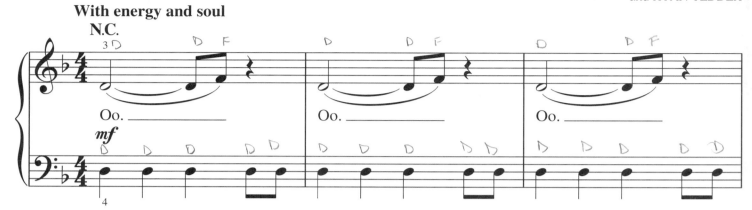

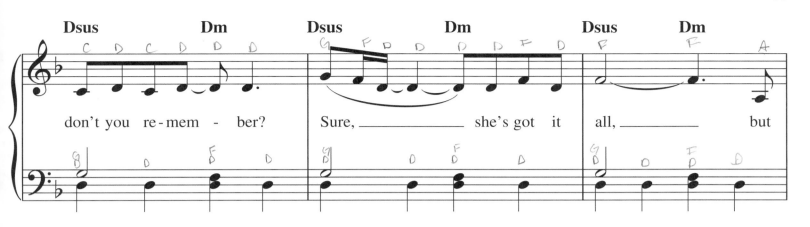

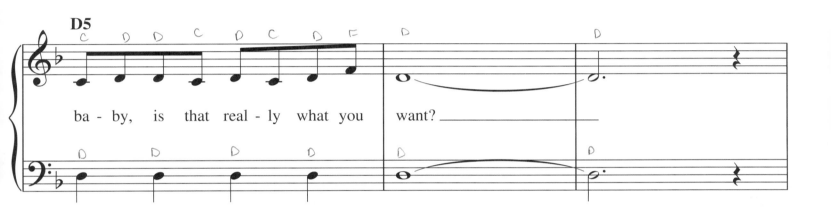

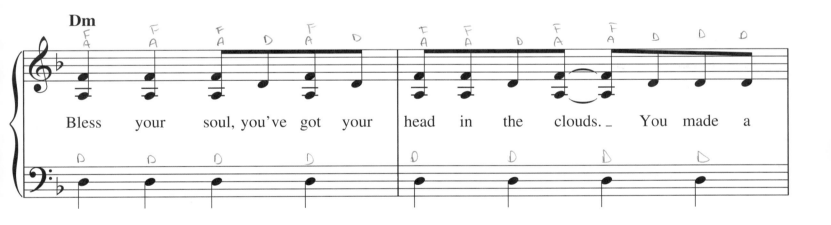

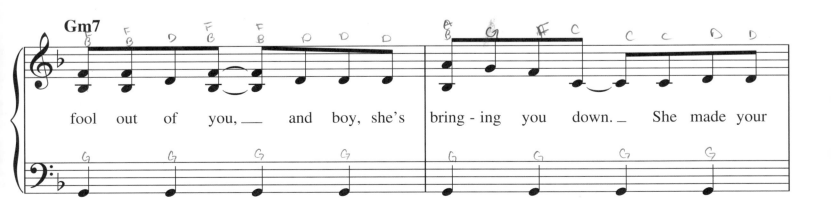

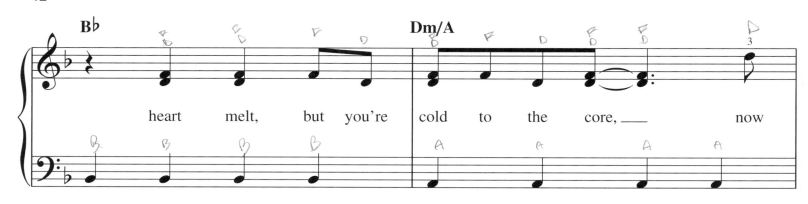

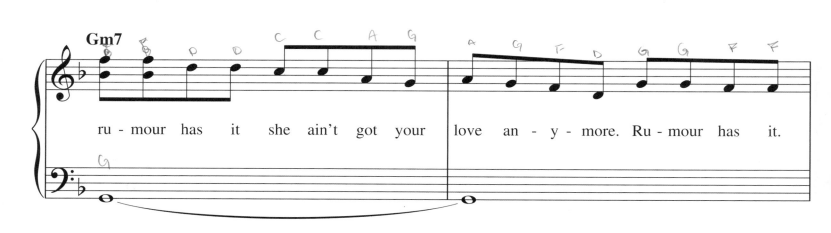

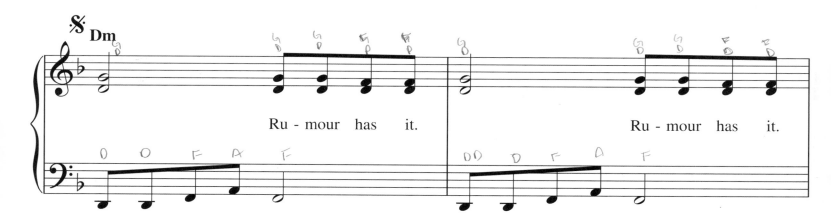

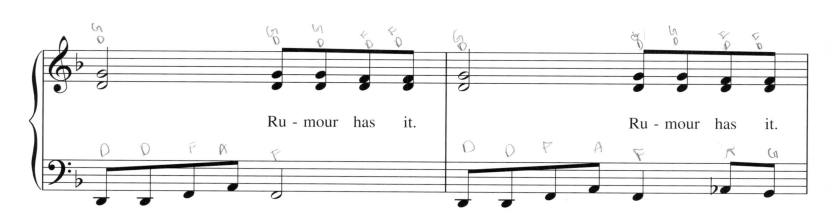

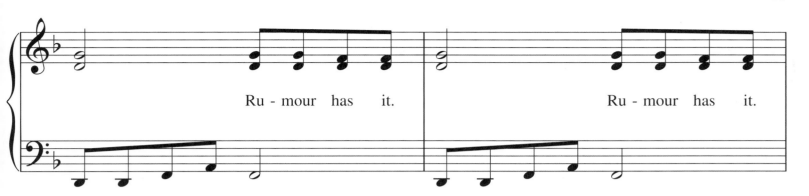

Ru - mour has it. Ru - mour has it.

To Coda ⊕

Ru - mour has it. Ru - mour. __

She _____ is half your

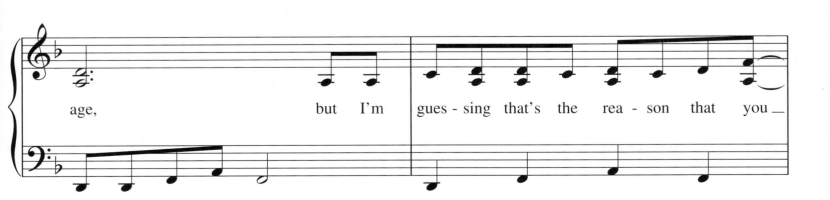

age, but I'm gues - sing that's the rea - son that you __

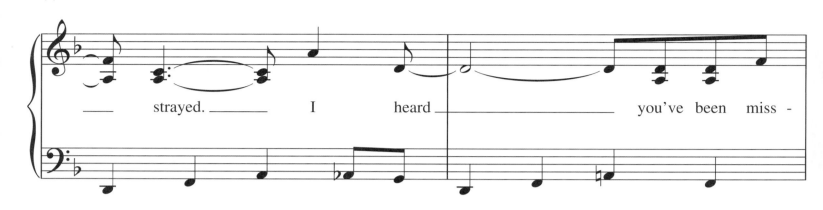

strayed. _____ I heard _____ you've been miss -

ing me. _____ You've been tell - ing peo - ple things you should - n't

be, _____ like when ____ we creep out and she ____

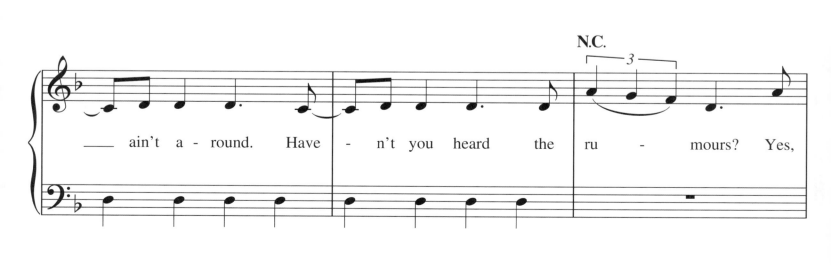

_____ ain't a - round. Have - n't you heard the ru - mours? Yes,

bless your soul, you've got your head in the clouds, __ you made a

fool out of me __ and boy, you're bring - ing me down. __ You made my

heart melt, yet I'm cold to the core, __ but

ru - mour has it I'm the one you're leav - ing her for. Ru - mour has it.

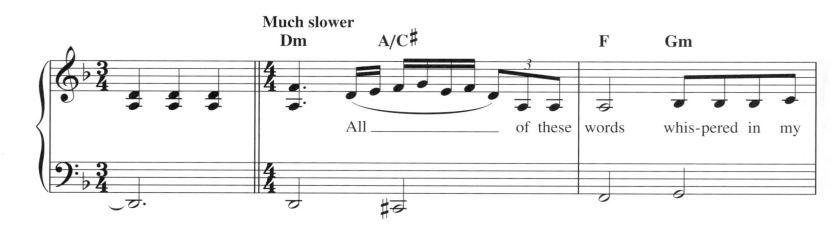

All _____ of these words whis-pered in my

ear tell a sto - ry that I can - not bear to

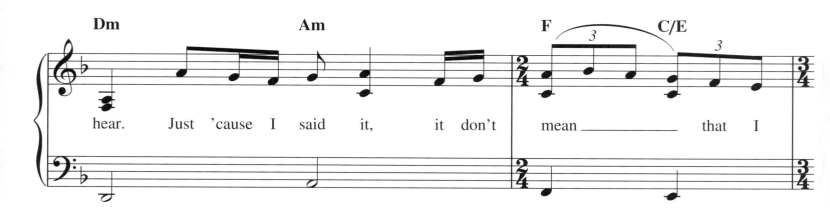

hear. Just 'cause I said it, it don't mean _____ that I

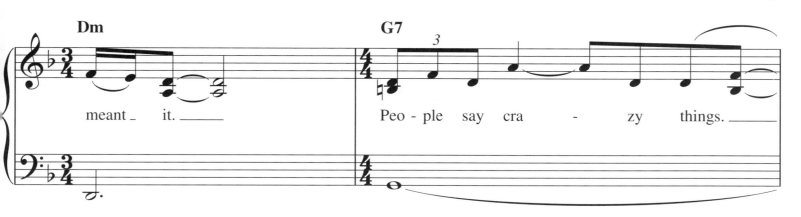

meant _ it. _____   Peo - ple say cra - zy things. _____

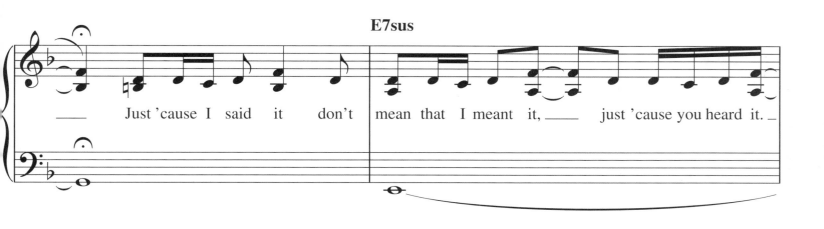

_____ Just 'cause I said it don't   mean that I meant it, _____   just 'cause you heard it. _

Ru - mour has it.

Ru - mour has it.   Ru - mour has it.

18

Ru - mour has it.   Ru - mour has it.

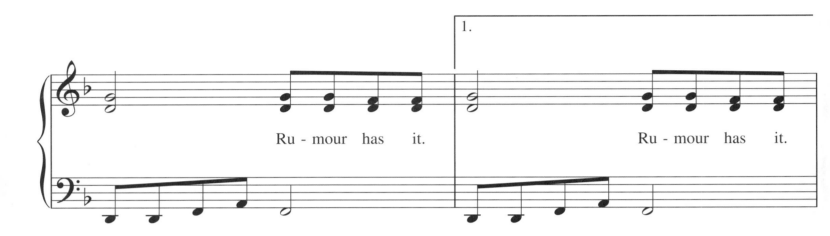

1.

Ru - mour has it.   Ru - mour has it.

2.

Ru-mour has it. Ru - mour.   Ru-mour has it.

Gm   **N.C.**   **Dm7**

Ru-mour has it he's the one I'm leav-ing you for.

TURNING TABLES

Words and Music by ADELE ADKINS
and RYAN TEDDER

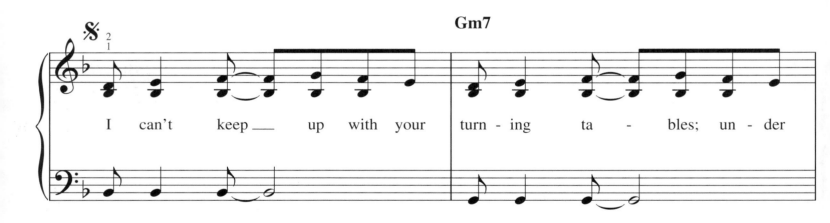

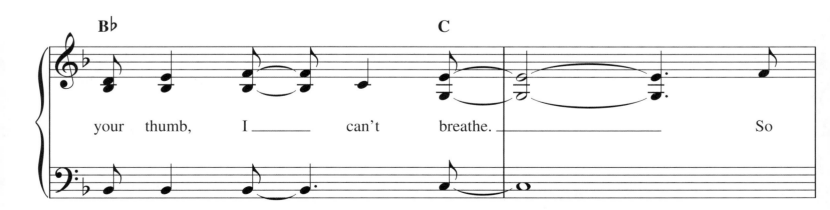

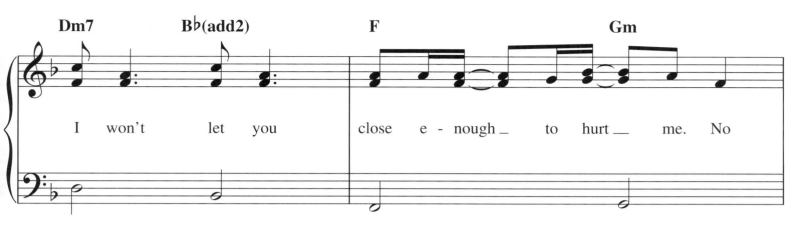

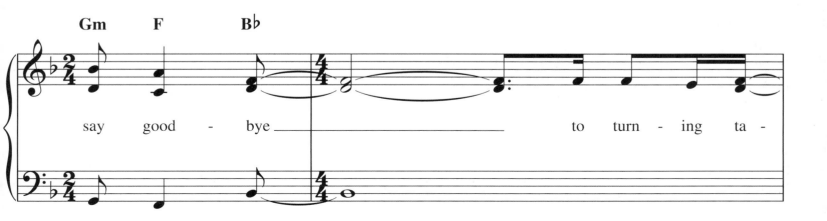

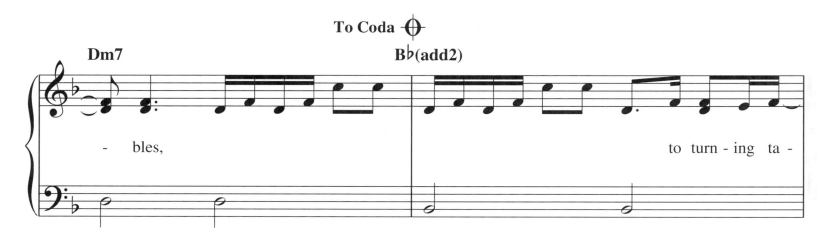

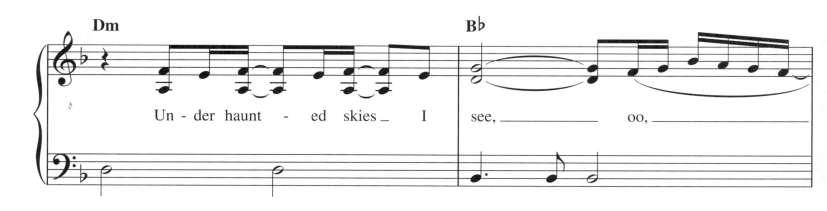

I braved a hun - dred storms __ to leave __ you, _____ as hard as you try, __

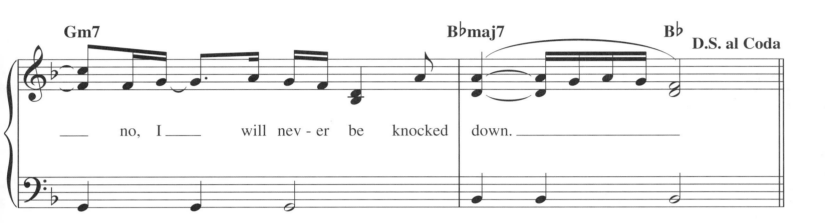

__ no, I ____ will nev - er be knocked down. _____

turn - ing ta - bles. __

_____ Next time, I'll ____ be brav - er,

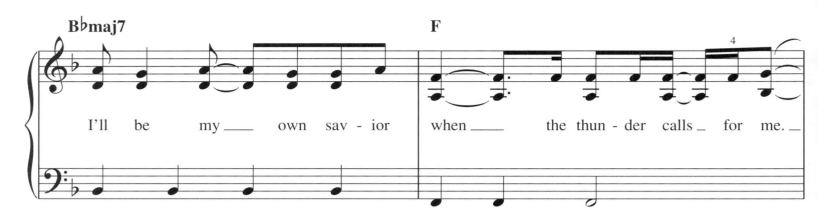

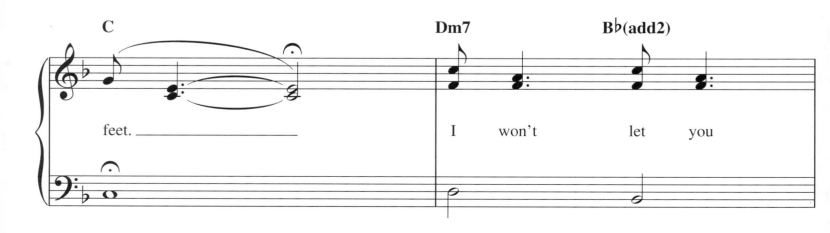

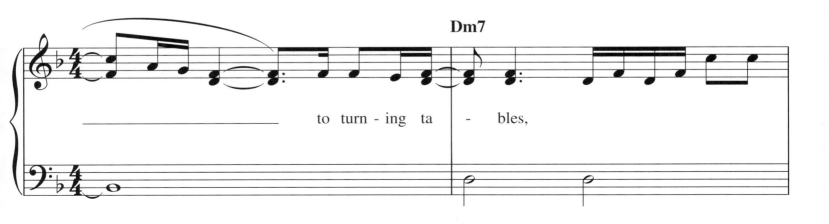

26

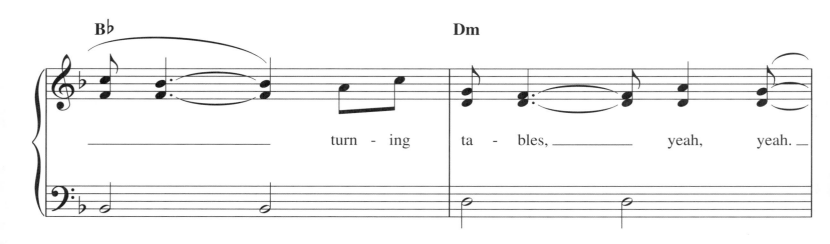

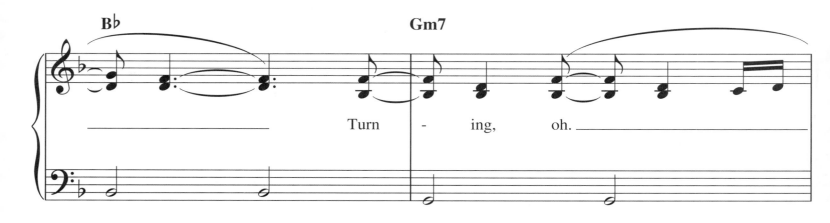

DON'T YOU REMEMBER

Words and Music by ADELE ADKINS
and DAN WILSON

Slow acoustic Ballad

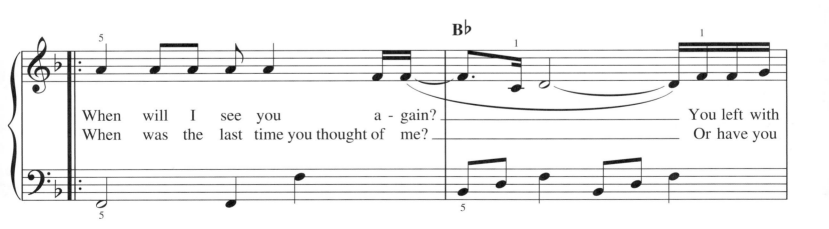

When will I see you a - gain? _____ You left with
When was the last time you thought of me? _____ Or have you

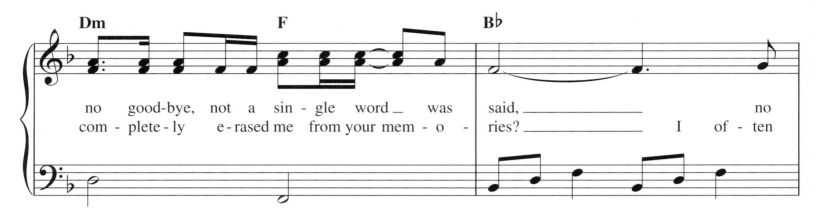

no good-bye, not a sin - gle word _ was said, _____ no
com - plete - ly e - rased me from your mem - o - ries? _____ I of - ten

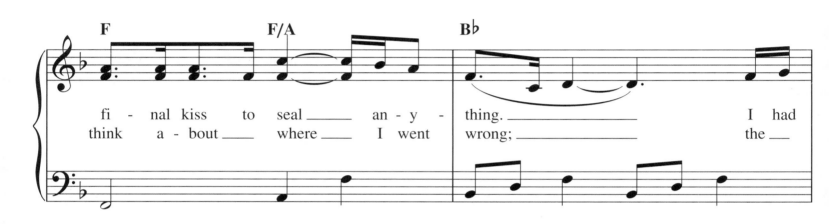

fi - nal kiss to seal _____ an - y - thing. _____ I had
think a - bout _____ where _____ I went wrong; _____ the _____

no i - dea of the state we were in. _____ I know I have a
more I do, the _ less that I know. _____ I know I have a

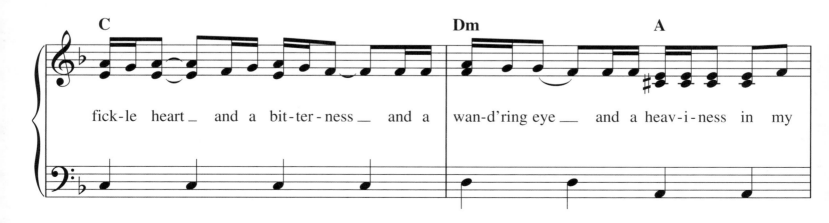

fick - le heart _ and a bit - ter - ness _ and a wan - d'ring eye _ and a heav - i - ness in my

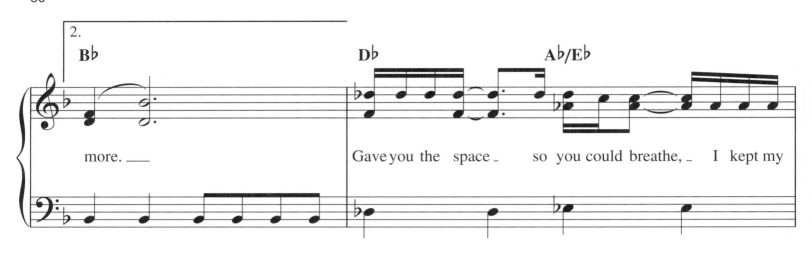

more. ___ Gave you the space __ so you could breathe, __ I kept my

dis-tance so you could be free. __ I hope that you find __ the __ miss-ing piece __ to

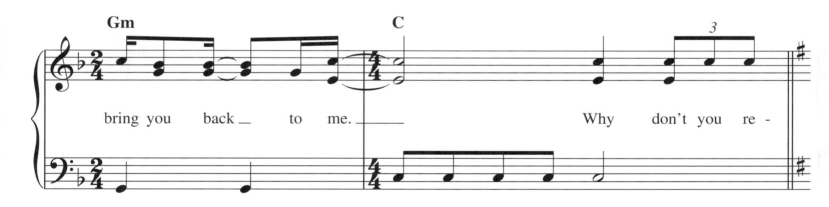

bring you back __ to me. ___ Why don't you re -

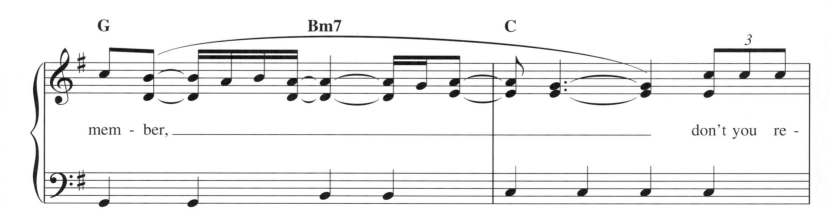

mem - ber, _____ don't you re -

SET FIRE TO THE RAIN

Words and Music by ADELE ADKINS
and FRASER SMITH

Pop Rock

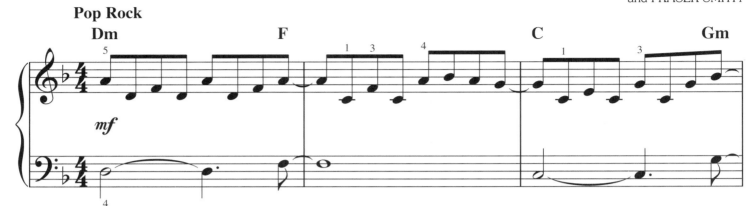

I let it fall, _____ my heart, _____ and as it

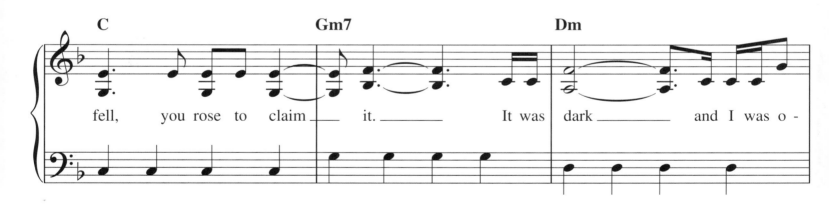

fell, you rose to claim _____ it. _____ It was dark _____ and I was o -

ver _____ un - til you kissed my lips _____ and you saved _____ me. _____ My

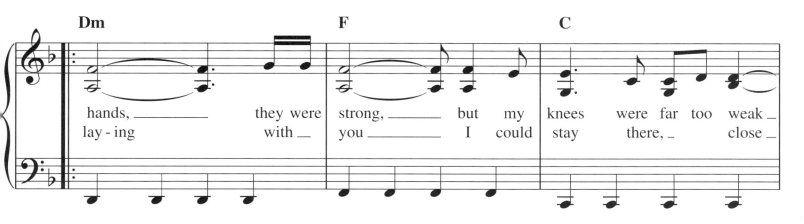

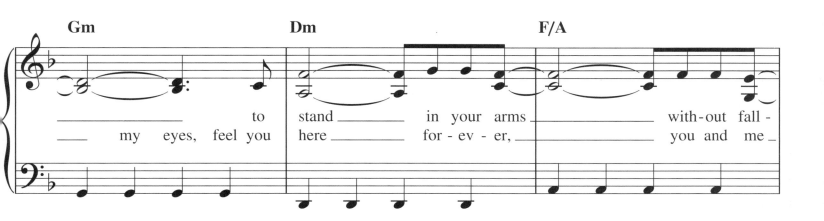

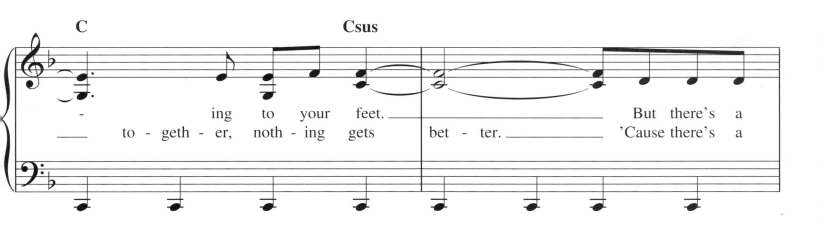

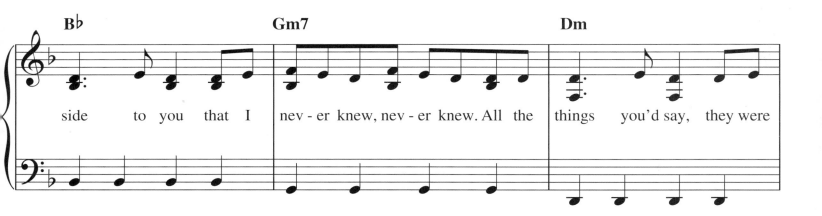

34

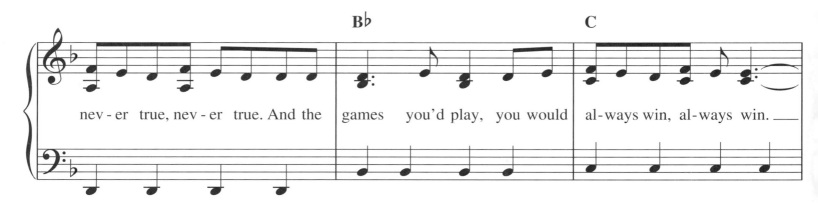

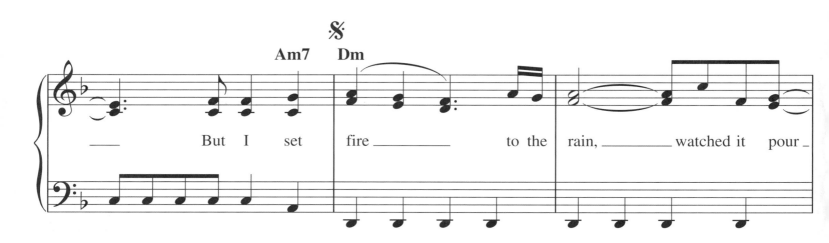

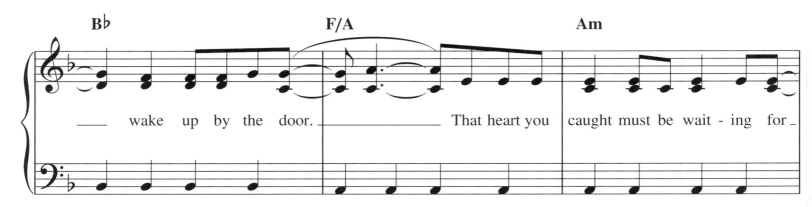

wake up by the door. That heart you caught must be wait - ing for

her. E - ven now, when we're al - read - y o - ver, I can't help

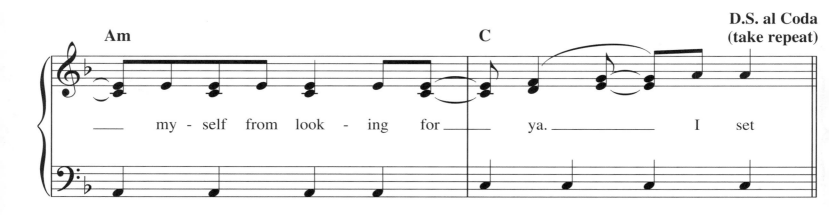

D.S. al Coda
(take repeat)

my - self from look - ing for ya. I set

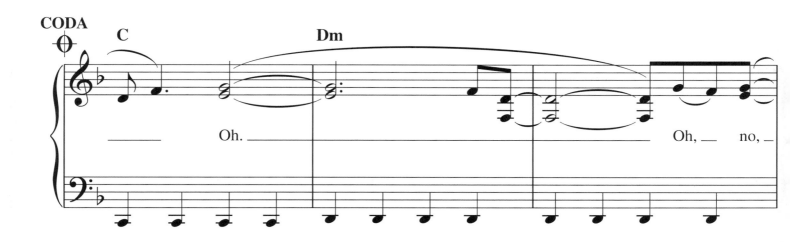

CODA

Oh. Oh, no,

HE WON'T GO

Words and Music by ADELE ADKINS
and PAUL EPWORTH

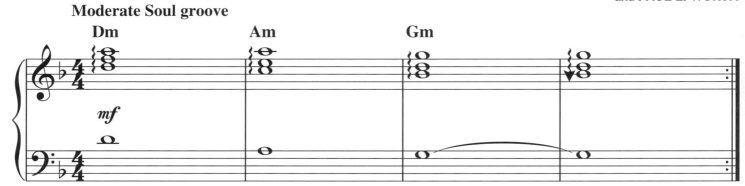

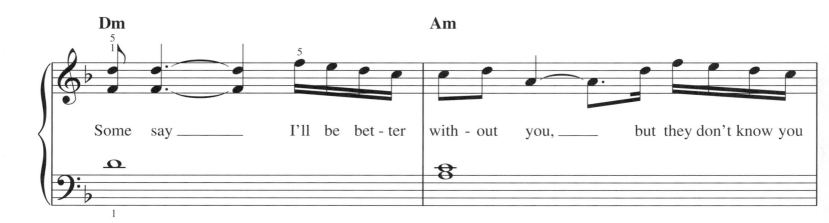

things I find, _____ like notes and clothes _ you've left be - hind. _

Wake me up, wake me up when all is done, _____ I won't rise un - til this

bat - tle's won, _____ my dig - ni - ty's be - come un - done. But I won't go, _____

_____ I can't do it on _ my own. _____ If this ain't love, then what is? _____

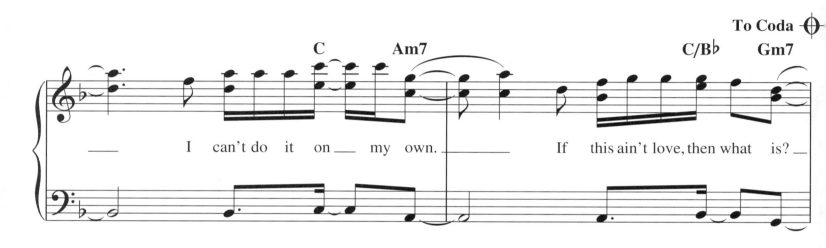

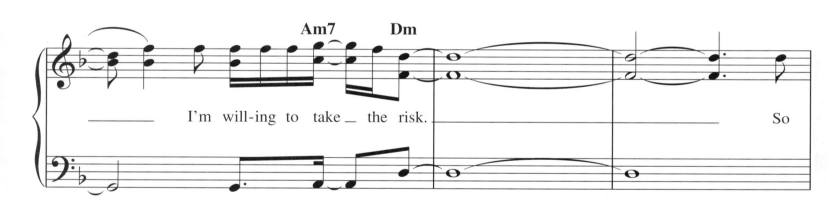

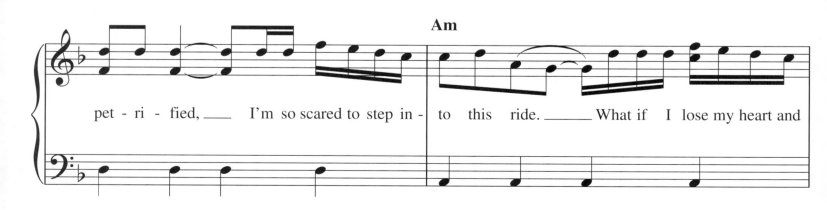

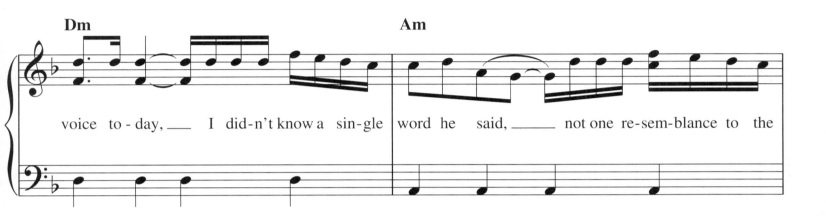

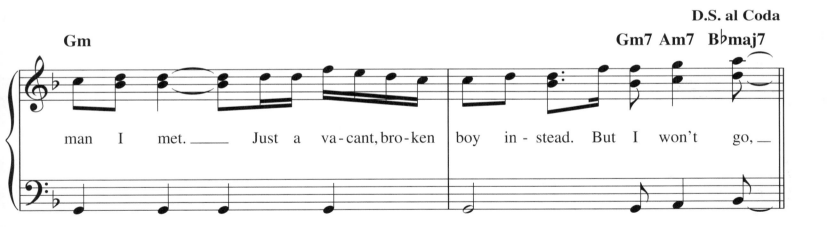

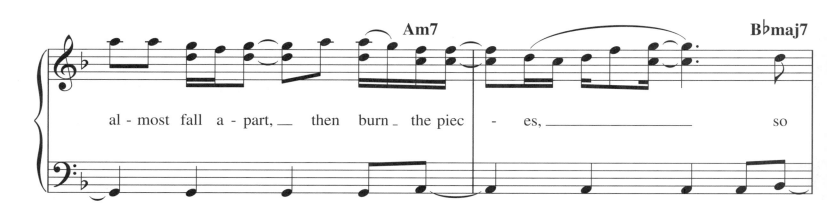

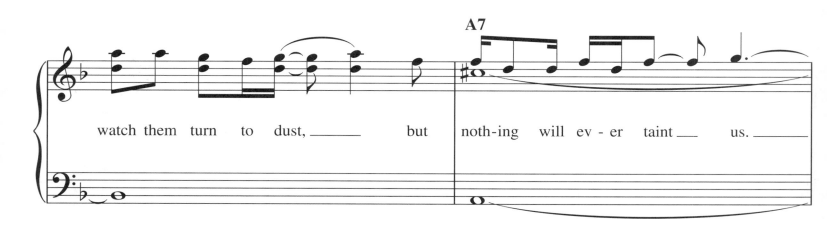

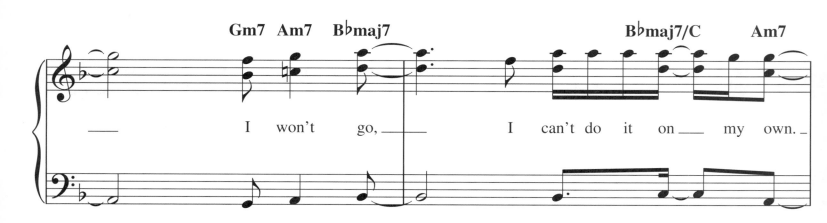

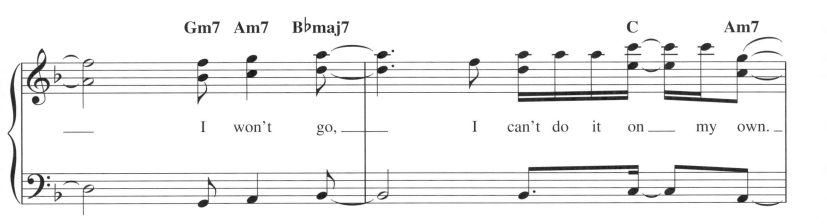

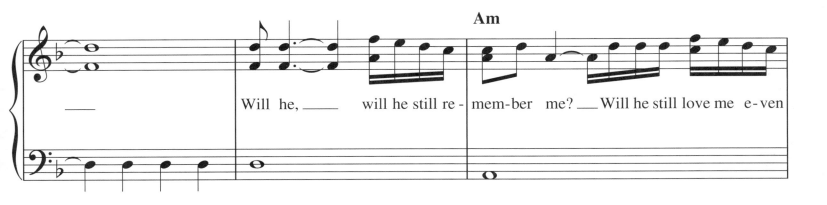

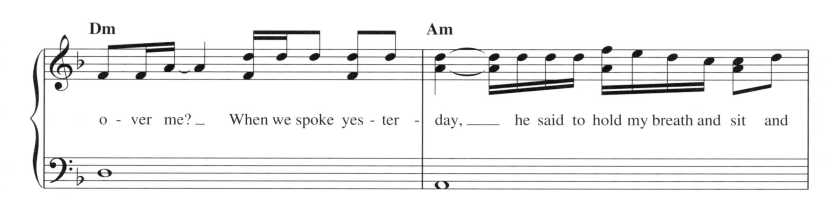

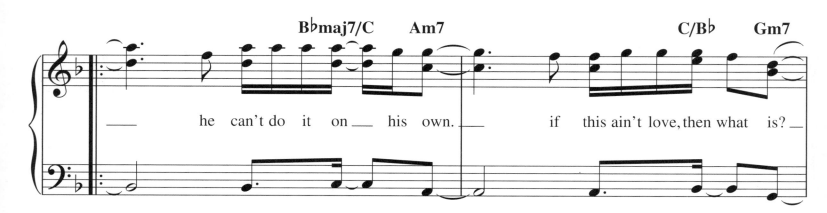

TAKE IT ALL

Words and Music by ADELE ADKINS
and FRANCIS EG WHITE

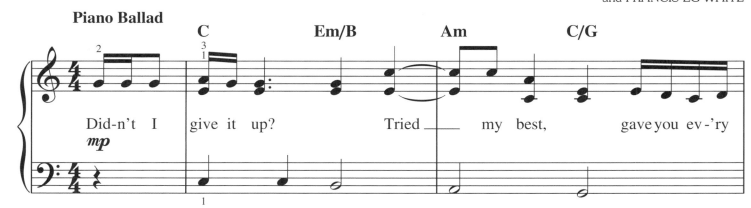

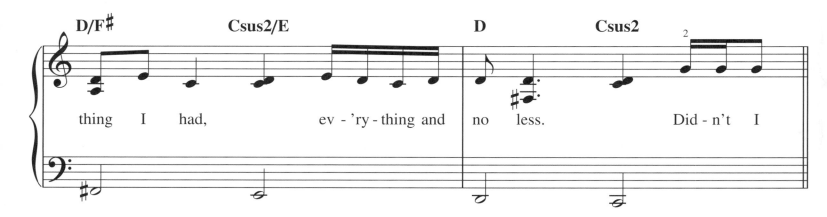

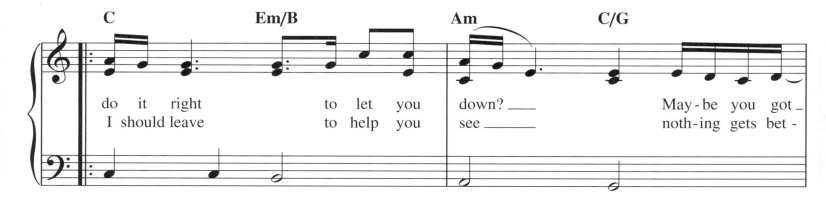

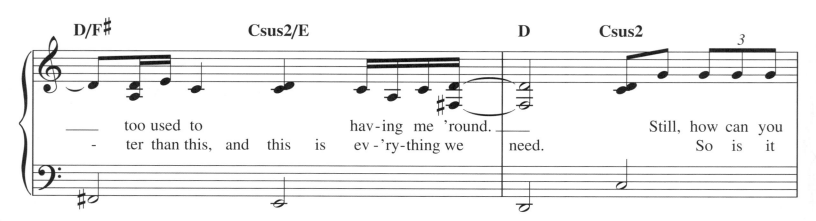

walk a - way __ from all my tears? ____ It's gon - na be an
o - ver? _____ Is this real - ly it? __ You're giv - ing up so

emp - ty road with-out me right _ here. But go on and
eas - i - ly, I thought you loved me more than this.

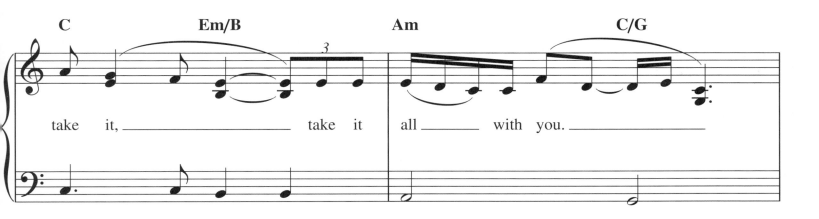

take it, _____ take it all _____ with you. _____

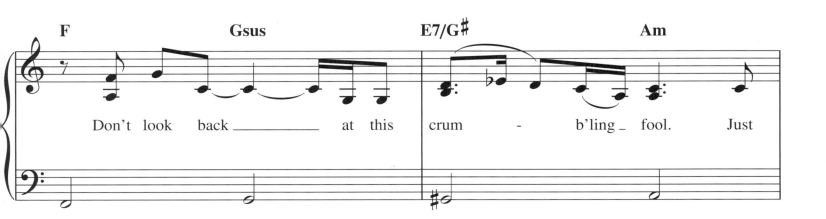

Don't look back _____ at this crum - b'ling _ fool. Just

48

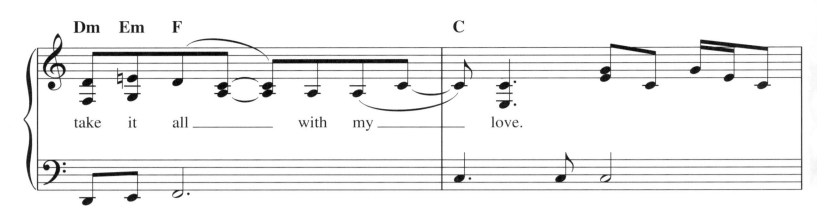

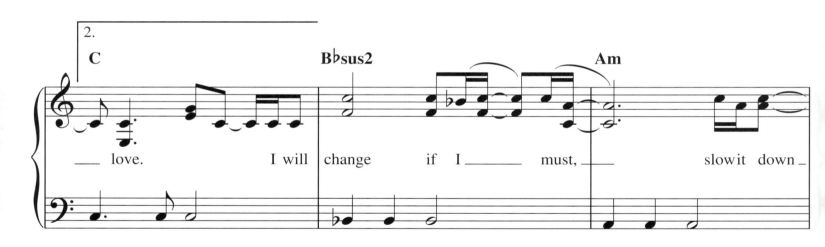

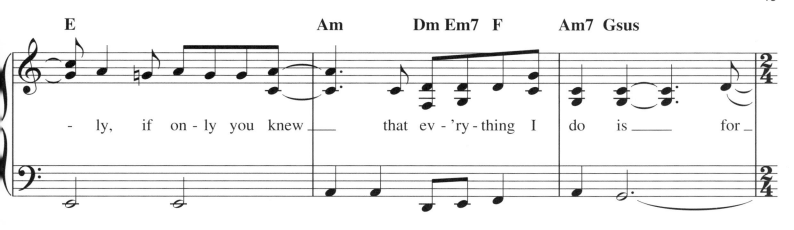

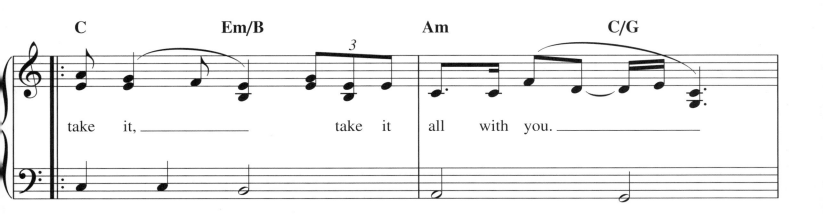

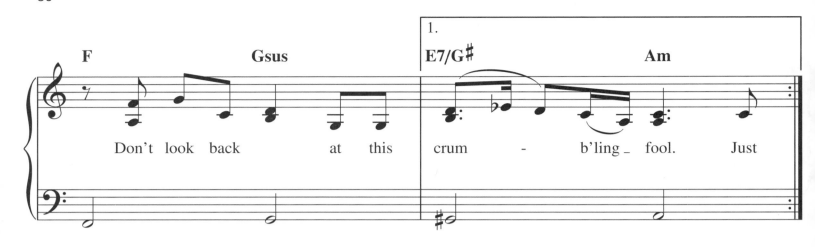

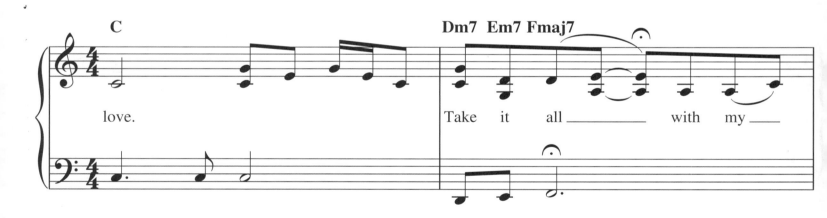

I'LL BE WAITING

Words and Music by ADELE ADKINS
and PAUL EPWORTH

52

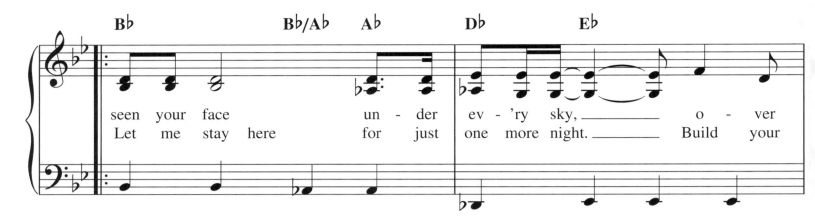

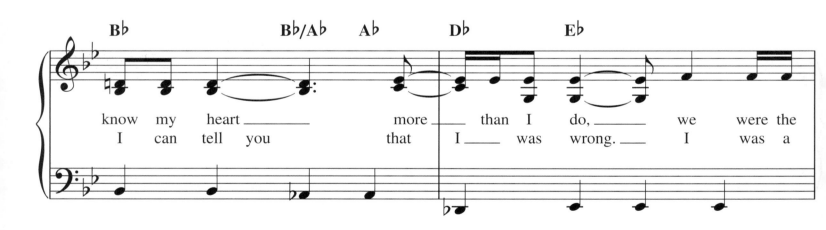

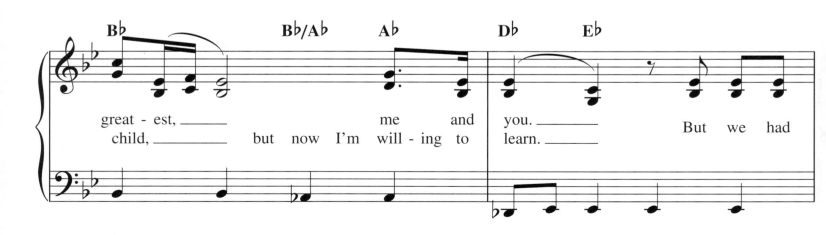

time a-gainst us and miles be-tween us, the heav-ens cried, _ I know I left you speech - less. But

now the sky _ has cleared and it's blue, _ and I see my fu - ture _ in you. I'll be

wait - ing for you when you're read - y to love me a - gain. _ I put my

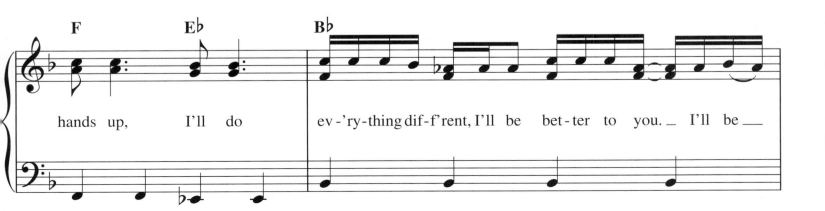

hands up, I'll do ev-'ry-thing dif-f'rent, I'll be bet-ter to you. _ I'll be __

54

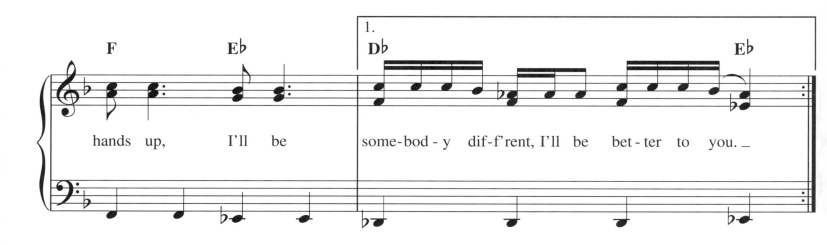

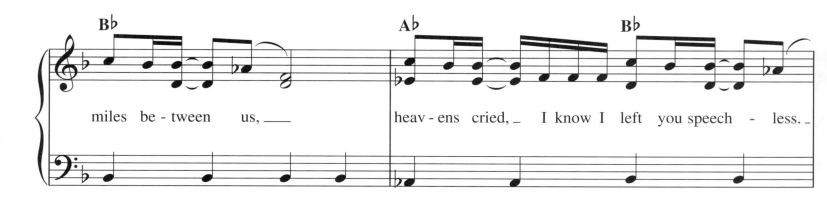

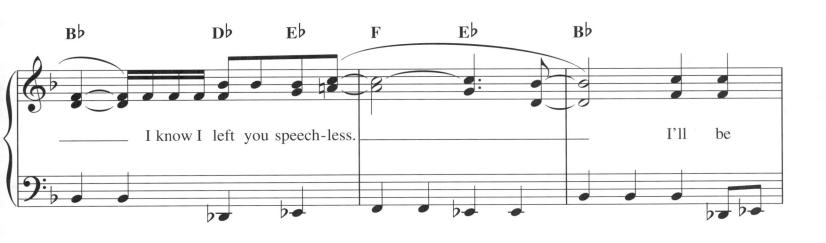

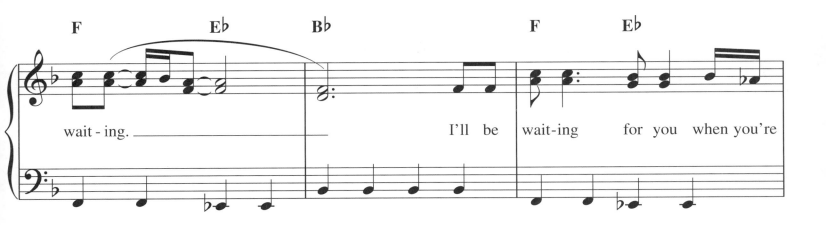

56

ONE AND ONLY

Words and Music by ADELE ADKINS,
DAN WILSON and GREG WELLS

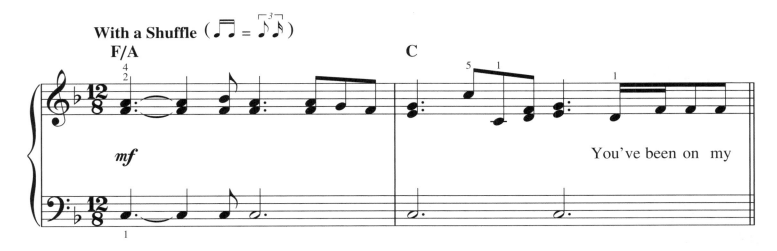

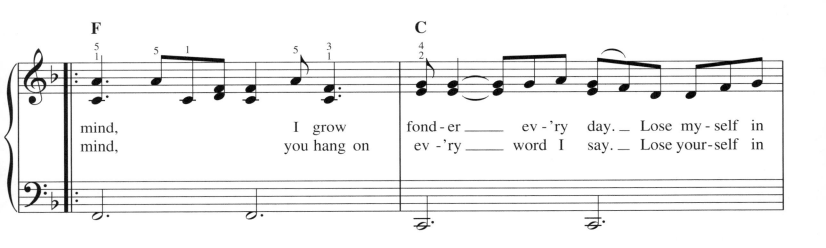

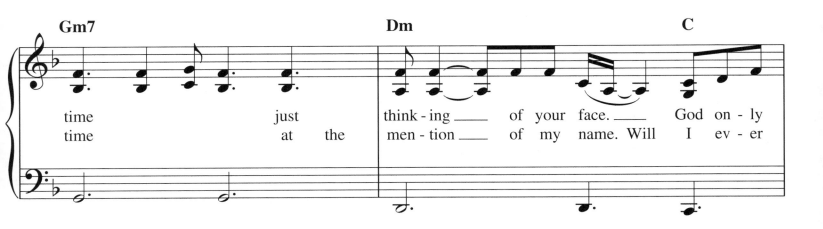

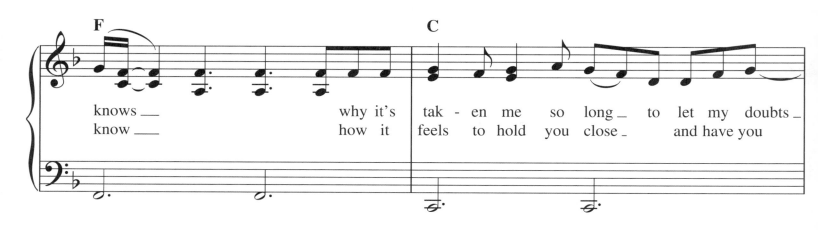

knows ___ why it's tak - en me so long ___ to let my doubts ___
know ___ how it feels to hold you close ___ and have you

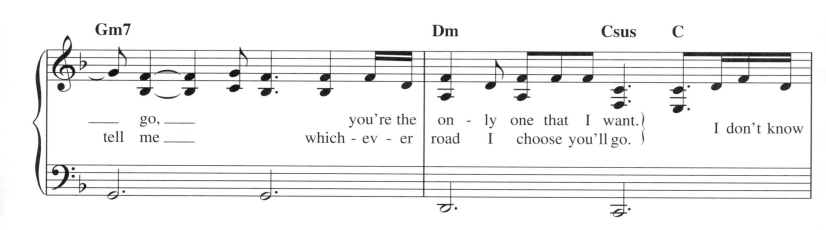

___ go, ___ you're the on - ly one that I want.
tell me ___ which - ev - er road I choose you'll go. } I don't know

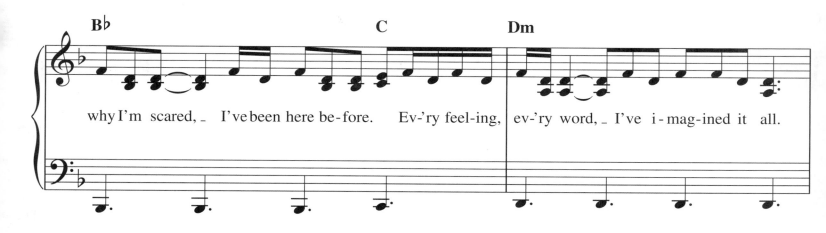

why I'm scared, _ I've been here be - fore. Ev-'ry feel-ing, ev-'ry word, _ I've i - mag - ined it all.

You'll nev - er know _ if you nev - er try ___ to for - get your past _ and sim - ply be mine.

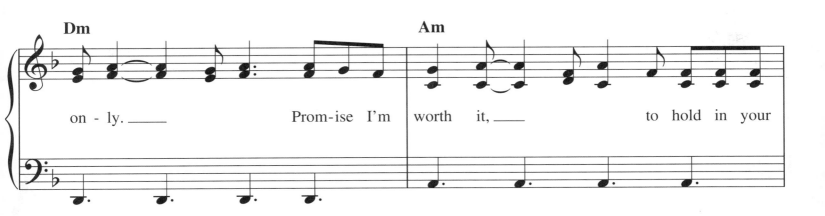

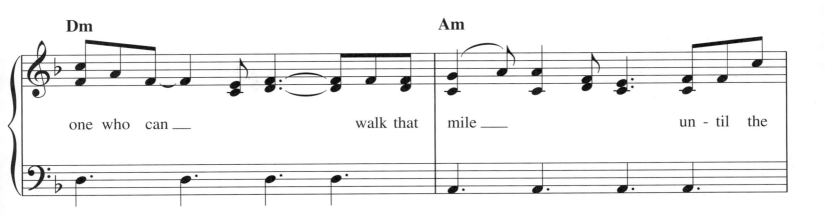

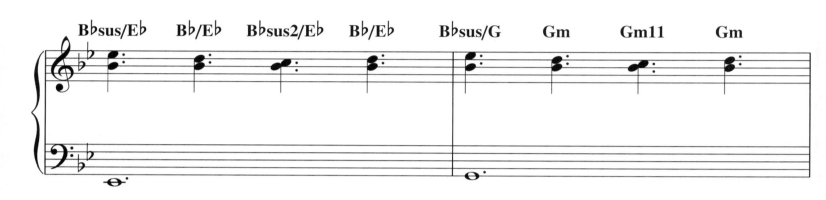

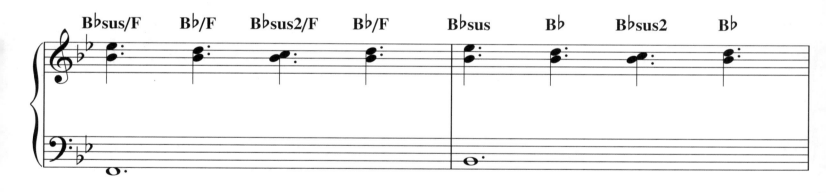

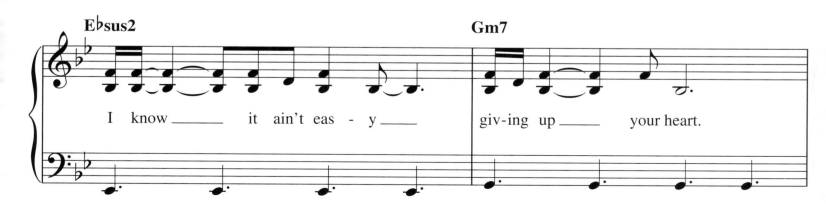

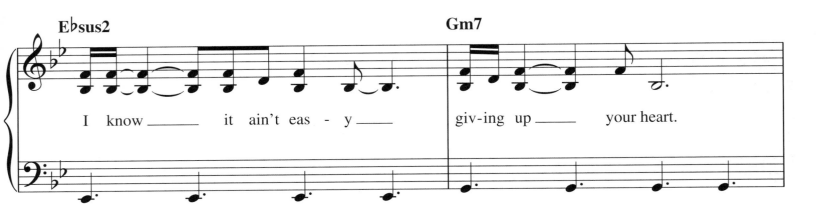

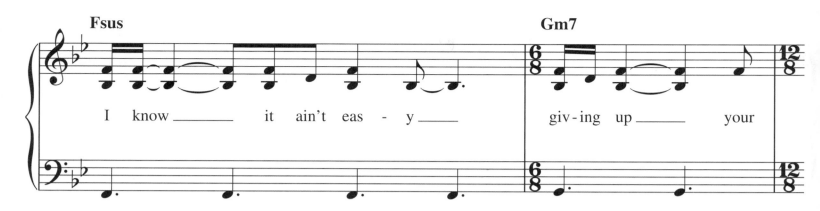

I know _____ it ain't eas - y _____ giv-ing up _____ your

heart. So, I dare you to let me be ___ yours, _ your one and

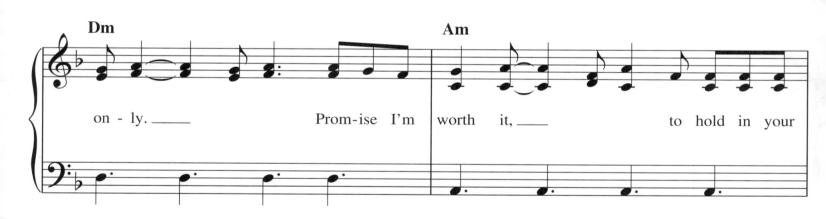

on - ly. _____ Prom-ise I'm worth it, _____ to hold in your

arms. So come on _____ and give me the chance _ to prove I am the

one who can ___ walk that mile ___ un - til the

end starts. ___ Come on _____ and give me a chance _ to prove I am the

one who can ___ walk that mile ___ un - til the

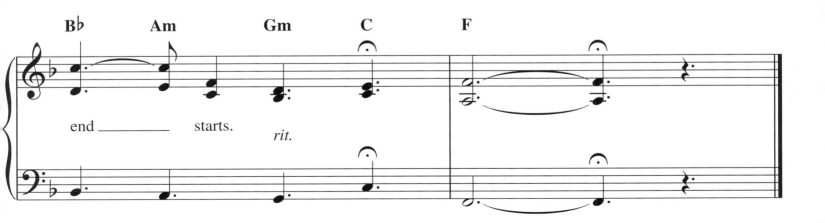

end _____ starts. *rit.*

LOVESONG

Words and Music by ROBERT SMITH,
LAURENCE TOLHURST, SIMON GALLUP,
PAUL S. THOMPSON, BORIS WILLIAMS
and ROGER O'DONNELL

Slow groove

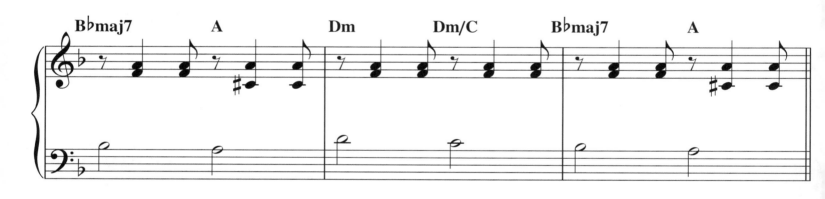

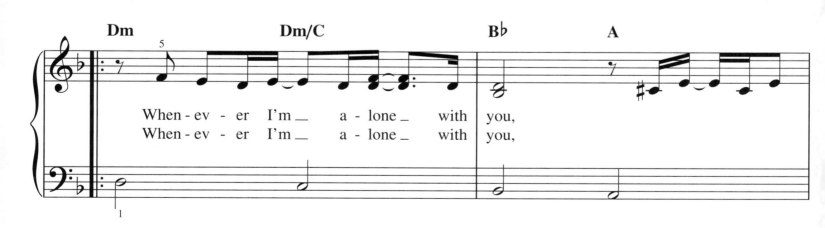

When-ev-er I'm __ a-lone __ with you,
When-ev-er I'm __ a-lone __ with you,

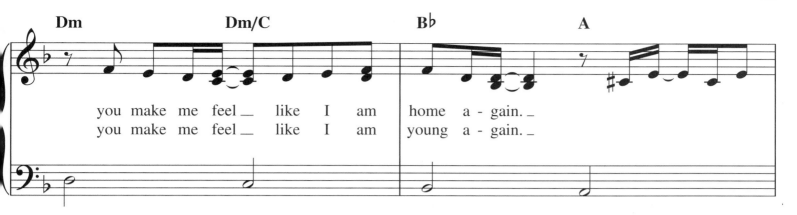

you make me feel __ like I am home a - gain. __
you make me feel __ like I am young a - gain. __

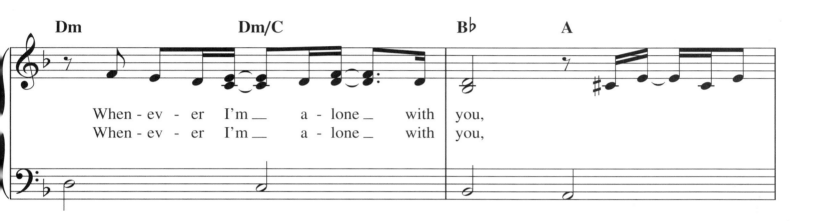

When - ev - er I'm __ a - lone __ with you,
When - ev - er I'm __ a - lone __ with you,

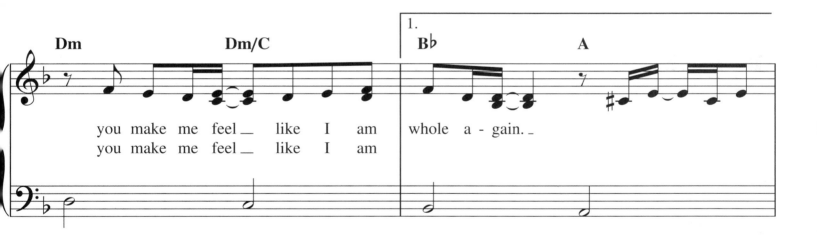

you make me feel __ like I am whole a - gain. __
you make me feel __ like I am

66

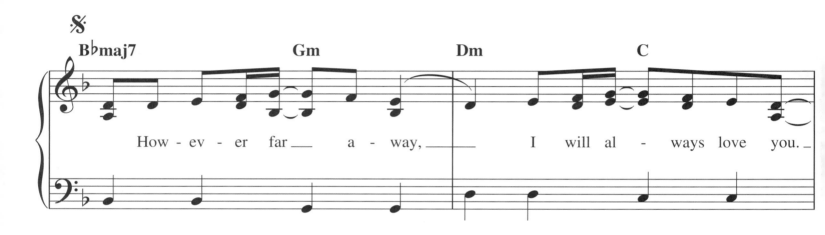

I will al - ways love _____ you.

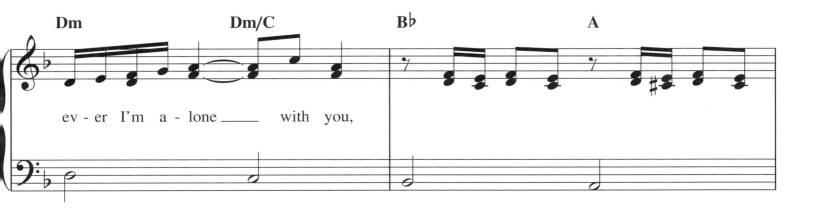

When -

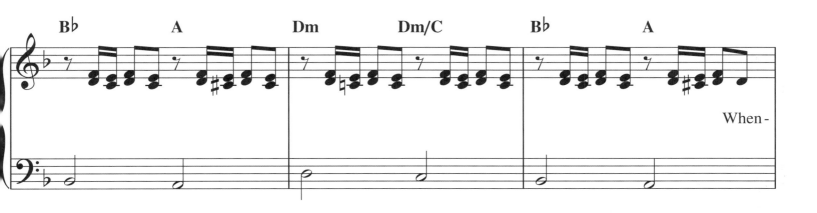

ev - er I'm a - lone _____ with you,

you make _ me feel _ like I am free a - gain. _ When -

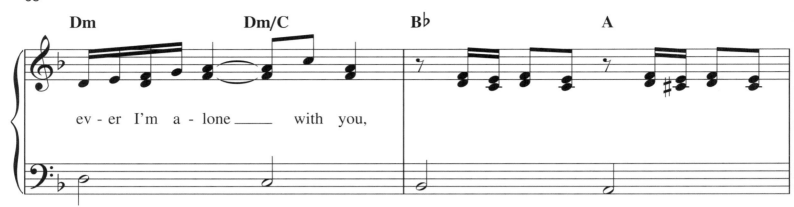

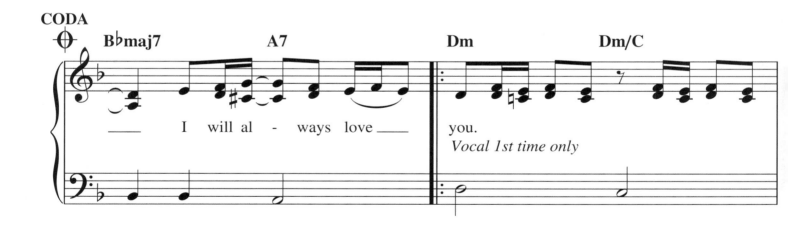

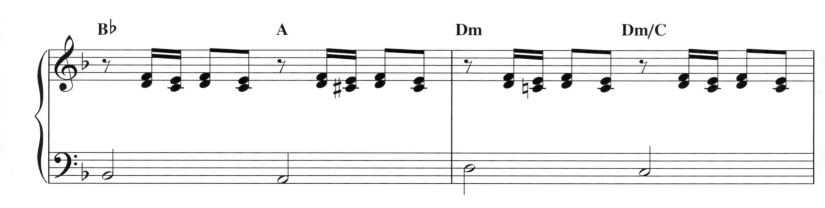

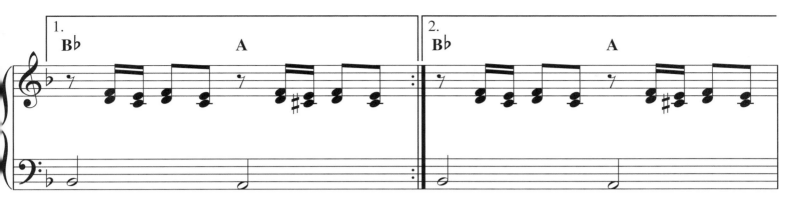

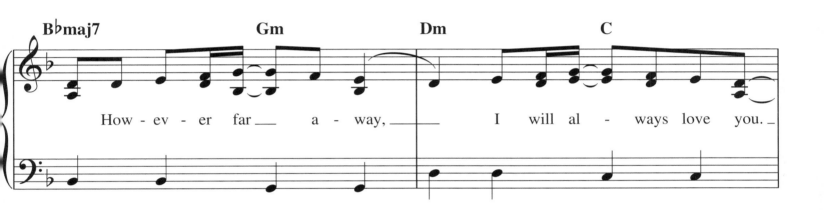

However far away, I will always love you.

However long I stay, I will always love you.

Whatever words I say, I will always love you,

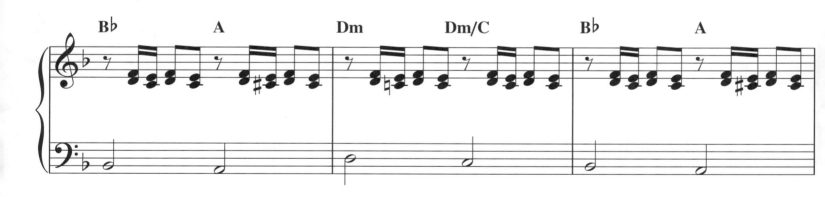

SOMEONE LIKE YOU

Words and Music by ADELE ADKINS
and DAN WILSON

72

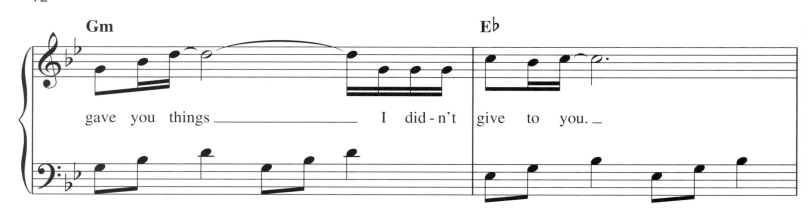

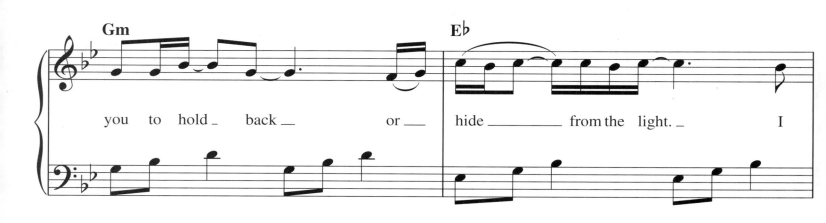

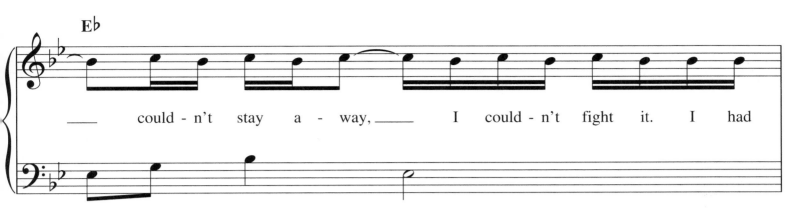

could - n't stay a - way, _____ I could - n't fight it. I had

hoped you'd see my face and that you'd be re - mind - ed that, for

me, _____ it is - n't o - ver. _____

Nev - er mind, _ I'll find some-one like you. I wish

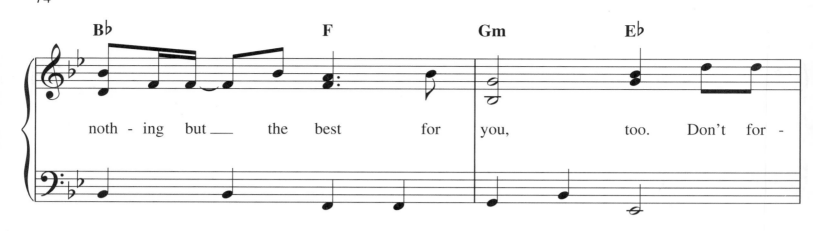

noth - ing but ___ the best for you, too. Don't for -

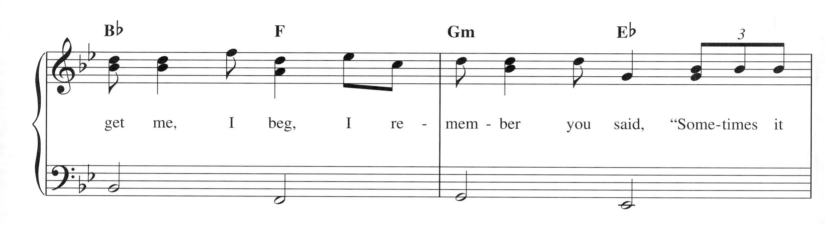

get me, I beg, I re - mem - ber you said, "Some-times it

To Coda ⊕

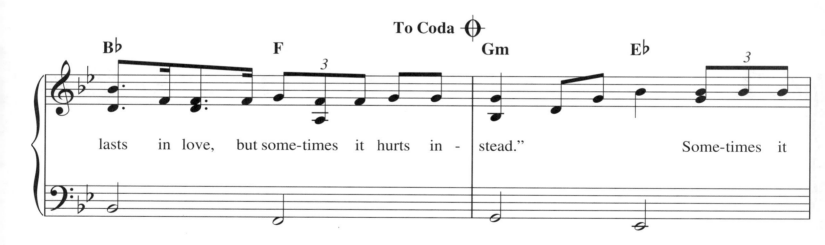

lasts in love, but some-times it hurts in - stead." Some-times it

lasts in love, but some - times it hurts in - stead. ___

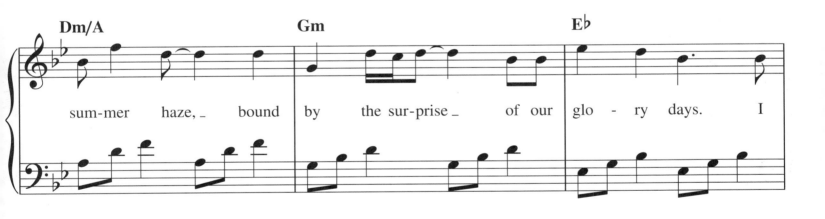

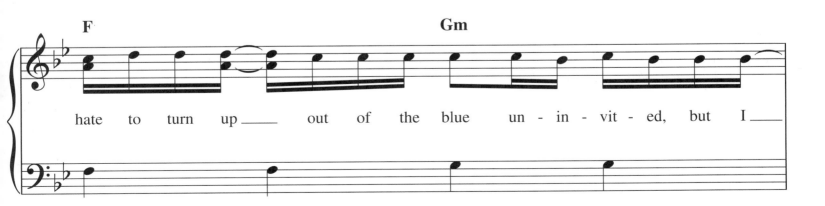

could-n't stay a - way, I could-n't fight it. I had

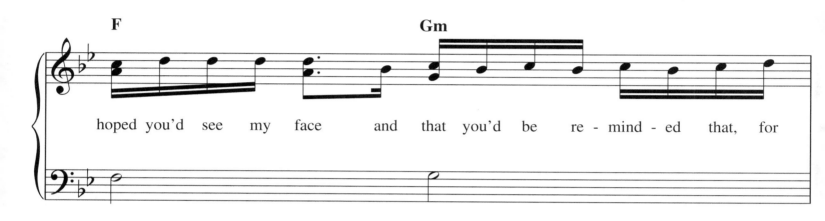

hoped you'd see my face and that you'd be re - mind - ed that, for

me, _____ it is-n't o - ver. _____

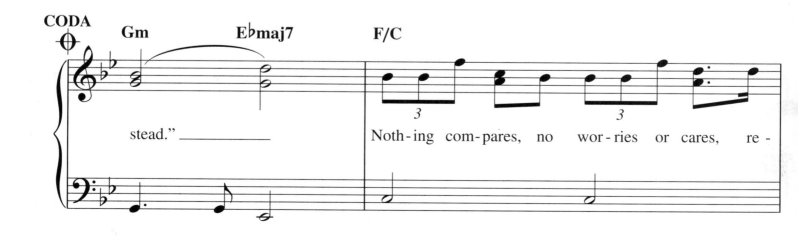

stead." _____ Noth-ing com-pares, no wor-ries or cares, re-

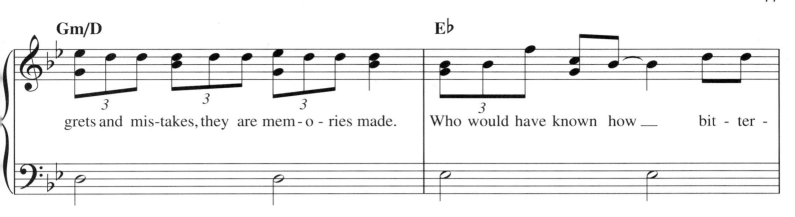

grets and mis-takes, they are mem - o - ries made. Who would have known how __ bit - ter -

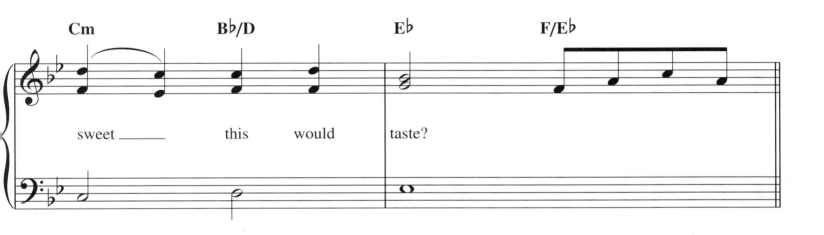

sweet _____ this would taste?

Nev - er mind, __ I'll find some-one like you. I wish

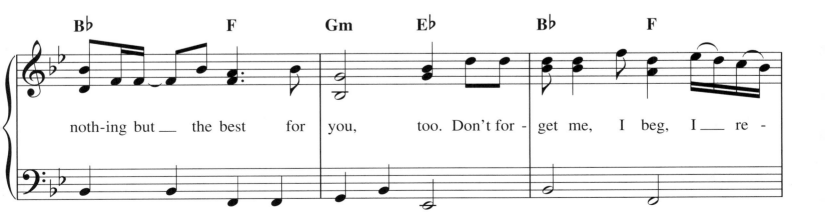

noth-ing but __ the best for you, too. Don't for - get me, I beg, I __ re -

78

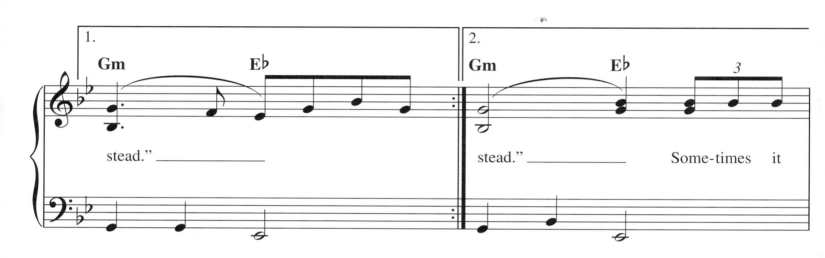

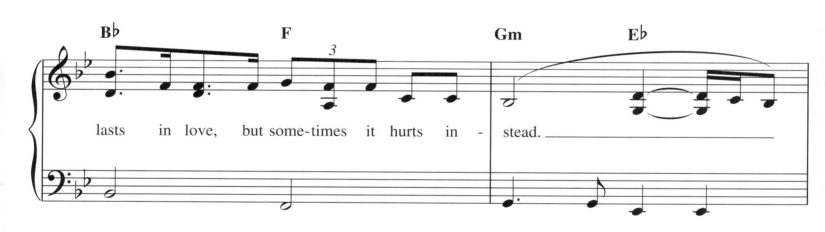